Original title:
A Jungle on the Shelf

Copyright © 2025 Creative Arts Management OÜ
All rights reserved.

Author: Julian Montgomery
ISBN HARDBACK: 978-1-80581-708-6
ISBN PAPERBACK: 978-1-80581-235-7
ISBN EBOOK: 978-1-80581-708-6

The Shelf's Wild Parade

In the corner, a sloth plays chess,
A turtle decides to wear a dress.
Parrots squawk in silly tunes,
Dancing disco under the moons.

Next to books, a lion naps,
While monkeys prank with funny claps.
A lizard, bright as a neon sign,
Sips lemonade, feeling mighty fine.

Cacti wear sunglasses, oh so cool,
While owls read rules of a silly school.
Frogs jump ropes with a jolly cheer,
While a bear spins tales with lots of beer.

On this shelf, oh what a sight,
Creatures frolic, pure delight.
Join the fun, don't take a shelf,
In this world, become yourself!

Between Pages and Petals

In the nook where the books reside,
Lies a tale with a playful stride.
A frog in a chapter, dressed in green,
Croaking laughs, a quirky scene.

Dust bunnies dance on a story's edge,
Over paper cliffs, they make their pledge.
With giggles echoing through old spines,
Every book's a joke that brightly shines.

Mossy Memories of the Past

Amidst the volumes, whispers creep,
Mossy thoughts that never sleep.
A worm with glasses reads aloud,
Every mischief draws a crowd.

Old maps curl in gentle pranks,
Treasure hunts with bookish flanks.
Silly shadows dodge the light,
In this realm, it feels so right.

Wild Literature in Quiet Corners

Papers rustle, secrets unfold,
In corners where stories are bold.
A cat in a tale, chasing the phrase,
Pounces on puns with a curious gaze.

Cricket symphonies fill the air,
As verses tumble in playful flair.
Each quote a giggle, a twist, a tease,
In a world where words move with ease.

The Secret Life of Literature

In the silence, the pages giggle,
Stories wiggle, making us wiggle.
A wise owl perches, laughs with glee,
As dragons nap, they dream of tea.

When humans leave, the plots run wild,
Fables frolic like a naughty child.
Bibliophiles in chaos caper,
In the twilight, a lively paper.

The Paper-Rooted World

In a land of paper vines,
Where every book's a quirky beast,
The lions laugh, the tigers dine,
As pages flip, they hold a feast.

Pencil trees in wild array,
With eraser blossoms sprouting wide,
A scribble critter leads the way,
To doodle dreams we cannot hide.

Echoes of the Wandering Wild

In the stacks, the whispers play,
Of monkeys swinging on the spines,
They trip and slip, hip-hip-hooray,
As chapters dance in sunny lines.

An owl hoots atop the lore,
As frogs croak tunes from jacketed tales,
Their ribbits echo, evermore,
In cozy nooks where laughter trails.

Stories Sprouted Anew

From margins grow a fearless crew,
A plot twist hints at wild delight,
With ink as food, they start to chew,
Creating mischief day and night.

The parrot's squawk, a bookish jest,
As paper planes take flight with flair,
Each story blooms and finds its quest,
In this wild world beyond compare.

The Shelved Safari

Take a ride on spines of books,
Through adventures, wild and bright,
With every nook, a giggle hooks,
Our laughter's echoing delight.

Giraffes peek down with silly grins,
While zebras dance on printed lines,
In our odd shelves, the fun begins,
Where all is wild, and none confines.

The Vivacious Veil

Among the books, a cover sways,
With tales of cats in funny ways.
A lion's laugh, a parrot's quip,
In this wild land, we take a trip.

The dictionaries dance in sheer delight,
As cookbooks juggle with all their might.
A romance novel twirls with flair,
While sci-fi robots claim the air.

Flora, Fauna, and Folklore

Vendor squirrels sell acorn hats,
While flower pots hold sassy chats.
Fables blink with mischief bright,
In garlands made of sheer delight.

Gardening gloves hold puppet shows,
Where tigers flaunt their funny bows.
A fox recites a haiku grand,
As orchids clap with gentle hands.

Illuminated by the Sunlight's Dance

When sunlight spills across the spines,
The shadows hint at silly signs.
A gnome, with swagger, takes a stand,
While cactus craves a rock band.

The chapters giggle in the breeze,
As figments tangle with the trees.
A dragon fries up tales anew,
While butterflies spin stories too.

Adventures Beyond the Spine

Between the pages, laughter reigns,
Where zebras ride on candy trains.
Koalas joke and drop their leaves,
As imaginary fun never grieves.

Pirates duel with feather pens,
While fairies gossip, grinning friends.
Epic quests and tales so grand,
In this giggle-filled wonderland.

Secrets in the Green Abyss

What's that plant doing with my shoe?
It's playing hide and seek, who knew?
A fern has donned a tiny hat,
With leaves that flail, it looks quite fat.

A vine swings low, it tries to dance,
I swear it winked, it took a chance.
A lizard laughs at my surprise,
In this leafy realm, the fun never dies.

Whispers Beneath the Canopy

The raccoons are gossiping it seems,
Sharing secrets in moonlit dreams.
A squirrel's made a tiny phone,
Chatter fills the air, none are alone.

Beneath the branches, giggles grow,
As owls throw shade with a wise, slow glow.
A rabbit's wearing glasses to read,
In this quirky world, they take the lead.

Sheltered Wilderness Unveiled

In this nook, a frog wears boots,
Practicing hops with some funky flutes.
A hedgehog juggles acorns with glee,
While the plants mock him mischievously.

Bunnies in pajamas dance at dusk,
Whirling 'round in a fragrant musk.
The fireflies applaud with tiny lights,
Creating a stage for these silly sights.

Tales of the Overgrown Hideaway

A sloth with wings, oh what a sight,
Claims he's a bird by day and night.
Swinging from branches in style so grand,
While the ants hold on with tiny hands.

The mushrooms gossip, cheeky and bright,
Sharing their tales underneath the light.
A caterpillar tries on a crown,
In this wild kingdom, who needs a town?

The Canopy's Embrace

In a nook with a view, creatures conspire,
Lions lounge while books catch fire.
A monkey flips pages, making a mess,
While owls wear glasses, feeling quite blessed.

Tigers sip tea, discussing their day,
While parrots tell tales in a comical way.
The giraffe struggles to reach for a tome,
As the otter insists it's like swimming at home.

Shelved Wilderness

Amidst the wood, there's quite a scene,
Where books become bushes, vibrant and green.
A zebra in stripes is reading a joke,
And the hippo just chuckles, almost to choke.

The tortoise holds court, wise and slow,
While frogs leap around in a talent show.
A cassette plays tunes from days gone by,
As squirrels make popcorn, oh me, oh my!

Echoes of Untamed Green

A parrot squawks loudly, "What's that I see?"
While a sloth just hangs, sipping his tea.
The butterfly buzzes with gossip so dear,
Mixing up facts, creating a cheer.

The wallaby winks, on a shelf made of pine,
And a hedgehog dances, feeling quite fine.
The rhythm of wildness, oh what a delight,
As lumbering bears inquire, "What's for tonight?"

Adventures in Paper Forests

In this forest of pages, the fun never ends,
With raccoons and rabbits all making new friends.
An armadillo rolls through, laughing with glee,
While the cat on the shelf decides to sip tea.

Beneath the bright leaves, the critters all play,
Creating mishaps in a joyful ballet.
A squirrel on stilts is causing a scene,
In this wild little world, pure chaos reigns supreme!

The Serpent of the Stacked Stories

In the corner, a python climbs,
Wrapped around books with strange rhymes.
Librarians think it's just a tale,
But it's plotting its next book sale!

Wiggly tales in stacks piled high,
With fables and legends that flutter and fly.
Each turn of the page, a sly little grin,
As the sneaky serpent dives right in!

Rooted in Fiction's Green

Among volumes thick, vines twist and twine,
Each title their own green, leafy design.
Characters chat from their lofty heights,
As grasses giggle in the bookish lights.

A squirrel in a novel pushes a cart,
Filled with acorns and truly charming art.
He claims he's the king of this leafy abode,
While hiding his stash where no one can go!

Nature's Palette of Old Tales

In this literary forest, colors collide,
Where plotlines bloom and humor takes stride.
The tales are painted, quite lush and bright,
As readers chuckle in sheer delight.

An owl in glasses reads with ease,
Wings flapping along with the bookish breeze.
Each whisper and giggle from branches above,
Tells of stories that we all love!

Hidden Canopy Chronicles

Beneath the dust, secrets unfold,
A canopy structured with stories retold.
Mice wear hats and recite their big dreams,
While the paper flowers dance in the beams.

Each shelf is a world, full of quirky sights,
With chattering raccoons under soft lights.
They jostle for space on the shelf so wide,
Laughing and playing with nowhere to hide!

The Lush Haven of Forgotten Dreams

In dusty tomes where whispers play,
A chameleon dreams the night away.
He wears a hat, quite tall and bright,
And dances with shadows in the moonlight.

The plants throw parties, lively and loud,
With orchids gossiping, feeling proud.
A sloth DJ spins the latest beat,
While vines make sure to keep it neat!

Old keyboards sprout into leafy trees,
As pillows sprout wings and float on the breeze.
There's laughter in corners, a curious sight,
When books share their secrets under starlight.

And though the spine cracks with every tale,
The laughter echoes, never to pale.
This haven of dreams, a quirky delight,
Where imagination takes off in flight.

Ferns and Fables Among the Pages

A fern once claimed to weave tall tales,
Of pirates who rode on broccoli sails.
The mushrooms chuckled, rolling their spores,
As books served tea on intricate floors.

One page turned into a shimmer surprise,
Where talking toasters had bright, laughing eyes.
They told of adventures through kitchen fog,
While beans played chess with the whimsical dog.

The grammar gremlins scribbled and danced,
While saucy characters eagerly pranced.
Each fable spun in colorful threads,
As the world of stories spun 'round in beds.

So, come sit down, share laughter and cheer,
In this land of ferns, no need for fear.
For every page has a story to tell,
In a garden where fables twist and swell.

Glimpses of Untamed Enchantment

In a corner, a cactus tells jokes so dry,
While butterflies giggle and teensy bugs fly.
They sip on dew like tea from a cup,
In a chaotic party where no one shuts up.

A lion's mane shimmies with rhythm supreme,
While whispering pages plot a strange dream.
Each leaf holds a secret, each petal a laugh,
As the whimsical life takes a curious path.

A clever old owl plays games with a fox,
Stealing wisdom from nails on the clocks.
With each tick-tock, a new joke appears,
And the room bursts out loud in unpredictable cheers.

So wander through brows with your eyes open wide,
In this land of mischief, where giggles reside.
While dogs and books share a shrug and a smile,
You'll find happiness hidden in each playful isle.

The Botanical Library of Shadows

Between the shelves, shadows sneak and play,
Chasing bright butterflies that flutter away.
A wise old fern tickles those who peek,
While witty puns make everything cheeky and sleek.

A pair of squirrels acts out their own show,
Reenacting grand tales with flair and a glow.
The spines start to creak with laughter and fun,
As tales intertwine under the setting sun.

Old cacti gossip about life out there,
Like a prickly social club that doesn't care.
Each pot holds stories of wild escapades,
Of chases through dreams in green masquerades.

So, dive into pages where enchantments flow,
With shadows as friends, and imagination aglow.
In this library of botanic might,
You'll find laughter lurking 'round every night.

Branches of Knowledge and Mystery

In the corner a creature peeks,
With glasses perched upon its beak.
A wise old owl, he clears his throat,
Points to volumes filled with a gloat.

Dust bunnies bounce like happy flies,
Chasing tales under watchful eyes.
The more you read, the more you find,
Stories twist with a goofy mind.

Cacti spin tales in pointy prose,
Each prick a giggle, just who knows?
Pages flutter, excitement's in tow,
As characters dance, stealing the show.

Smiles sprout from every spine,
Witty jokes woven like a vine.
In every nook, laughter thrives,
Branches shake where the funny survives.

Where Pages Blossom with Life

Among the leaves, a frog does sing,
In a top hat, he's quite the thing!
With each turn, a laughter swells,
Where stories bloom like playful spells.

A cat in boots, struts down the line,
With a rapscallion dance, oh so fine.
He flips the script with a purr and a spin,
Finding mischief where tales begin.

Inky vines wrap tales so tight,
Every plot twist a merry fright.
With worms in caps, they plot and scheme,
In a world woven from a dream.

Petals giggle, pages sigh,
As rhymes take flight into the sky.
With every leaf that flutters free,
Life's a laugh, just wait and see!

The Flora of Forgotten Verses

In dusty books, the flowers bloom,
Petals whisper secrets in the gloom.
A daffodil reads with a smile,
While daisies dance, just for a while.

Tangled tales stuck in spider threads,
Giggling gnomes peek from their beds.
Each word a sprout in this quirky patch,
With laughter growing in every batch.

Mushrooms pop with tales of yore,
Knocking on pages, asking for more.
Fun creeps in with a bounce and a jig,
As learners laugh and tease the pig.

Vines of verse twist in delight,
Shadows play in the fading light.
In forgotten words lies playful cheer,
A garden of humor waiting near.

Twisted Roots of Imagination

Roots stretch wide, entwined and bold,
Inwards grow stories yet untold.
A vine of whimsy, a twist in time,
Where fantasies bubble in rhythm and rhyme.

Squirrels debate the best nutty plot,
As they scurry and scamper, they laugh a lot.
With a pinch of fun and a dash of game,
Each twist reveals a new wild claim.

Quirky creatures peek from their lair,
Magical mischief hangs in the air.
With roots that jiggle and shake and sway,
Imagination dances, all night and day.

Whether it's laughter or whimsy-filled dreams,
In each turn of the page, joy gleams.
From twisted roots to branches above,
In this playful forest, there's nothing but love.

The Enchanted Thicket

In a thicket of books, there's a tree,
With squirrels that dance and chatter with glee.
They jig on the spine of an old, worn tome,
While whispers of wisdom come calling them home.

A raccoon in a coat reads a tale of the sea,
And two owls debate who's the wisest, you see.
They hoot with delight, causing quite the ruckus,
As a fox in a scarf shows off his new circus.

The Wild Within Pages

On pages of parchment, a giraffe does glide,
He stretches his neck, with dictionary pride.
A lion in slippers leads a book club too,
Debating the plots of what's fanciful and true.

The pages all giggle as bugs steal the show,
While ants in tuxedos put on a grand show.
With a flip and a flap, the wild things ensue,
In this curious realm, where laughter rings true.

Ferns and Fables

Amid the green ferns, a frog shares a joke,
His laughter erupts, between each puff and croak.
A beetle in glasses tells tales of the past,
While a worm in a top hat thinks everything's vast.

The crickets all chirp in a chorus so bright,
As owls wield a quill, writing stories at night.
Each fable unfolds as the stars twinkly beam,
In this whimsical space, where nothing's as it seems.

Leaf-Laden Lore

Under bright leaves, a snail spills the tea,
On gossiping petals, of florals that flee.
A chipmunk recites tales of mischief and fun,
While butterflies dance 'neath the illuminating sun.

The stories unfold with each turn of the leaf,
And laughter resounds, easing worries and grief.
In this charming bazaar where stories intertwine,
Every moment a treasure, each moment divine.

Stories in the Underbrush

In the thicket where shadows play,
Squirrels tell tales of a giant ballet.
They leap and they spin, what a sight to behold,
Nuts in their pockets, their stories unfold.

The frogs keep a ledger, a gossip so bold,
Of snails racing turtles, a tale to be told.
With laughter and ribbits, the bamboo shakes,
While giraffes cackle, as the hedgehog quakes.

Little ants plot with a crumb as their prize,
A feast that would open the biggest of eyes.
But watch out for the squirrel, quite crafty, my friend,
He'll swipe the last piece, and that's how it ends.

The crickets all chirp in a hilarious jam,
While the owls, they hoot, "This is quite an exam!"
So gather your friends, let the fun not be shy,
In this tangle of tales, we'll all learn to fly.

Whispers from the Canopy

High above the ground, where the monkeys swing,
They critique the fashion of the birds who sing.
"Your feathers are lovely, but how do they fare,
When it rains on your style, is there water in there?"

The parrot retorts, "Well, I'm bright and I'm bold,
Unlike your patchwork or drapes that are old!
Last Tuesday, I counted my compliments thrice,
While you're stuck on branch with a nut for your price."

The tallest of trees whisper secrets and laughs,
As the pinecones debate on the best types of staffs.
A squirrel in plaid claims the title of king,
While the branches applaud, it's a jubilant fling!

So listen closely, and you might just hear,
A symphony of banter, with joy, not with fear.
In the heights of the green, let your worries all fade,
Join the chatter above, where wild stories are made.

Chronicles of the Wild and Wise

In the thickets so dense where mischief resides,
A wise old tortoise offers up guides.
"Tread light on the grass, my sprightly young friend,
Or you'll startle the critters who just want to blend."

A raccoon then pipes up, "But I love to explore!
I rummage through bins, oh, I'm quite the folklore!
Each trashcan has treasures, and half of it's gold,
My stories of mischief, worth more than they're sold."

The owls always chuckle at tales of the day,
When the hedgehog donned glasses and thought he could play.
"Let's dance," he declared, but he tripped on his feet,
Now he rolls down the hill—oh, isn't life sweet?

So gather your friends for the chronicles deep,
In this forest of laughter, where memories leap.
With every turn, let your spirits run free,
In the wild and the wise, let's all just be we.

The Color of Secrets

In the hush of the leaves where the secrets are spun,
The critters conspire, oh what fun to be done!
The parrots gossip, "What shade shall we wear?
Magenta or yellow? The brightest, we dare!"

A chameleon chuckles, "Oh, let's mix them all,
I'll be polka-dots through this colorful ball!
On a Tuesday I'm orange, by Friday I'm blue,
Mysteries shimmer in every hue."

The butterflies laugh as they flit to and fro,
"You've no secret costume, so what do you show?"
The lush hues of nature join in a parade,
As the flowers all sway, in vibrant charade.

So sprinkle your laughter like paint on a screen,
In this riot of colors, let your heart glean.
Keep your secrets close, but don't shy from the blend,
For life's a grand canvas, on which we all spend.

Petals of the Past

In dusty books, the roses hide,
With tales of bees that lost their pride.
A war of thorns, a flower's jest,
Petals whisper secrets, oh what a fest!

Vines tangled with stories, so bizarre,
One book's a tree, another, a star.
Laughter echoes through the leaves,
As mice recite what the old tome weaves.

The Untamed Archive

A parrot squawks from history's shelf,
While laughing crickets read of themselves.
Tigers duel with a pair of socks,
In a chaos of stories, they throw off their locks.

Dust bunnies dance with every plot twist,
Chasing tales that no one could resist.
Squirrels scribble, plotting their schemes,
While time on the shelf bursts at the seams.

Fables Written in Green

Once a frog held court in a book,
Wearing a crown from a shady nook.
Toads sang ballads, slick and sly,
As trees cracked jokes with the wind nearby.

Fables of ferns and spores so bold,
Each page a treasure, a whimsy to hold.
Silly stories in a leafy hue,
Where laughter sprouts like morning dew.

Life Between the Shelves

Among the tomes, soft giggles rise,
Chameleons dream of rainbow skies.
An owl juggles a few old tales,
While snails surf through dusty trails.

On every shelf, a story unfolds,
With hiccuping vines and marigold molds.
Crickets and spiders throw a grand ball,
In the library's heart, they have a great call!

The Wild Around the Words

In a book, the beasts do play,
They flip through pages, night and day.
With hats and coats and shoes to wear,
They dance and prance without a care.

A lion roars, a monkey swings,
While page by page, the laughter sings.
A parrot squawks a joke to share,
And every tale has laughter rare.

The scribbled notes are trails of fun,
Where rhymes are chased and puns just run.
A gopher grins, a turtle winks,
In this wild land, no one thinks!

So dive right in, don't miss the thrill,
Each chapter's a party, if you will.
Among these creatures, joy awaits,
In wild adventures, love abates!

Leaves of Imagination and Lore

The leaves are turning, stories grow,
With twists and turns in every row.
They rustle softly, secrets told,
In wacky whims that shine like gold.

From fairy wings to dragon tales,
A boat of words with mighty sails.
The branches stretch, and minds will soar,
In each new tale, there's always more!

Squirrels chime in with cheeky rhymes,
While hedgehogs dance in whimsical climes.
The stories jump from tree to tree,
With laughter bouncing wild and free.

So grab a leaf, come take a read,
In books, dear friend, there's joy guaranteed.
The leaves may whisper, twist, and twirl,
An open book? A whole new world!

The Secret Garden of Literature

In this garden, tales grow tall,
With every plot twist, hear the call.
The flowers giggle, colors bright,
In this wonderland, pure delight!

A butterfly tells jokes with flair,
As bees buzz softly, unaware.
The daisies whisper, 'Join the spree!'
While vines twist round in jubilee.

Rabbits read with glasses perched,
Each paragraph, a flower searched.
With every line, the laughter blooms,
Amidst the wild with sweet perfumes.

So step right in and smell the prose,
In this garden, every word glows.
Adventure waits with silly sprites,
In stories crafted, pure delights!

Syllables Amidst the Lianas

Among the lianas, words swing free,
With syllables dancing a jubilee.
Each letter bounces from leaf to leaf,
In jungle tales, delight, not grief!

A wordy parrot jumps on a vine,
Chiming in with a joke that's divine.
The chittering monkeys craft a rhyme,
In this merry dance of bookish time.

A lion's roar creates a rhyme,
While typos bloom like fruit in prime.
And laughter echoes in every nook,
As squirrels write lines in a storybook!

So swing with joy on syllable swings,
In this vibrant world, where laughter rings.
A jungle of fun, come take a peek,
This wild wordplay is what we seek!

Nature's Ink on Shelves of Stories

In the corner of the room, a vine creeps,
Books like trees, where the imagination leaps.
Each spine a trunk, with stories to tell,
Laughter echoes, under the leafy spell.

Fictional birds chirp in poetic delight,
Pages fluttering softly, taking flight.
A monkey named Mark swings from the top,
While tales of adventure never seem to stop.

Inkwells bubble like a bubbling brook,
Characters peek out, come take a look!
A zebra in a suit reads out loud,
As giggles ripple through the leafy crowd.

Oh, the wild things that live in this space,
With random quips, it's a vibrant place.
Nature's mischief spills from every shelf,
As stories grow, led by laughter itself.

Lost Tribes of the Literary Forest

Deep in the pages, a tribe doth dwell,
Wearing bookmarks like hats, oh what a swell!
They dance on the words, with a jolly sound,
In this land of scribbles, where joy is found.

With paper mache shields and inked-up spears,
They battle dull moments, conquer our fears.
A sage named Scribble chants tales of fun,
While giggling at grammar under the sun.

They feast on wild prose and rhyming fruit,
Laughter in leaves, in their playful pursuit.
Plot twists like trails, they blindly explore,
In the wild literary lore that we adore.

These tribes of jesters, with creative zest,
Remind us all that laughter is the best.
With each turn of the page, a new gag awaits,
In this forest of fiction, joy radiates.

Beneath the Underbrush of Thought

Under the thicket where the stories sprout,
Words wiggle around, hopping about.
A peculiar squirrel collects all the verbs,
While hidden puns peek out from theurbs.

The whispers of wisdom tickle the leaves,
Dreams take the form of cheeky reprieves.
Imaginations dig in like roots of a plant,
Spreading their giggles, helping us chant.

A rabbit named Rhyme hops here and there,
Telling tall tales with a comedic flair.
The underbrush rustles, ideas collide,
As laughter blooms bright, we cannot hide.

In this quirky haven where thoughts intertwine,
Ink spills with joy, creating lines divine.
Life's little chuckles rise like the sun,
Beneath all the hedges, we find our fun.

The Habitat of Ink and Growth

In a cozy nook where the wild things play,
The ink runs free, in a colorful sway.
Wordy weeds grow thick with giggles and grins,
In this verdant space, everyone wins.

A hedgehog named Haiku rolls through the prose,
While a raccoon, named Reader, munches on those.
Stories sprout like flowers, each having their say,
In this lively habitat where whimsy holds sway.

The plot thickens like pudding, rich and profound,
With characters lurking all over the ground.
A cacophony of chuckles, a riotous scene,
Adventure's the juice in this foliage green.

So gather 'round, share a laugh at the shelf,
For nature's humor thrives alongside itself.
In the habitat of ink where ideas take flight,
The joy of the journey makes everything bright.

Verdant Whispers in Quiet Corners

In a nook where the ferns sway,
Books are busily plotting their play.
Monkeys in stories chase after the words,
While frogs recite poems, leaping like birds.

Lizards wear glasses, reading in style,
Cockatoos joke and turn pages awhile.
Each spine holds secrets, beneath leafy dreams,
In the hush of the shelf, laughter softly teems.

A parrot suggests a wild book club,
Where every reader gets a belly rub.
With vines as bookmarks, they swing and they sway,
In this cozy retreat, who wouldn't want to stay?

Under the covers, the stories come alive,
With whispers and giggles, the books high-five.
In the soft glow of evening, they swap silly tales,
Just a jungle of laughter, where friendship prevails.

Prose Among the Petals

In a corner where daisies softly spill,
A sonnet is brewing, with giggles to thrill.
The petals all flutter, listening close,
As fiction gets flirty, and the humor grows.

Bees join the chorus, buzzing with glee,
Telling tales of a wise old bumblebee.
He wrote a book on sweet nectar's best brew,
But claimed all the honey was stolen—oh boo!

With rhymes weaving in like vines in a wave,
Every stanza is cheeky, with puns to save.
A trickster in petals shares a cheerful rhyme,
As laughter cascades like a free-spirited chime.

In this garden of words, where the funny buds sprout,
Prose blooms with joy, that's what it's about.
A picnic of laughter, all ages partake,
In the petals of prose, sweet memories we make.

Rhymes in the Green Light

Under ferns, in the glow of a sunbeam,
Words frolic and follow like a playful dream.
Bouncing and giggling, they trip on their lines,
Creating a ruckus where sunlight entwines.

A squirrel scribbles verses with a chic little quill,
While caterpillars ponder their poetic thrill.
Each rhyme is a riddle, each line is a tease,
In the merry chaos, they do what they please.

Crickets are crooning, their chorus on cue,
With grass blades a-twirling, in dances so true.
A chuckle erupts from a wise old owl,
As punchlines land softly with a comical growl.

Between leaves of laughter, the stories expand,
In the green light, they make quite a stand.
A carnival of words, where jokes never end,
In the rhymes of the green, there's always a friend.

The Leafy Reverie of Written Worlds

On the shelf, where the wild things reside,
Each book has a secret it's keen to confide.
A caper ensues as the pages all wiggle,
With plot twists so silly, they make the leaves giggle.

With a tangle of tales that twirl and that twist,
A parakeet grins, not a word to be missed.
Each chapter's a party, each footnote a dance,
In the leafy delight, word wizards prance.

The stories get cheeky, the narratives bold,
As the ink spills adventures waiting to be told.
A snail slows the action, keeps time with a rhyme,
Every twist and turn is simply sublime.

In the attic of laughter, these fantasies dwell,
With whimsy and wonder, they weave their own spell.
A realm of sweet mischief on each papery stage,
In this leafy reverie, turn every page!

Harbored Tales in the Thicket

In a thicket thick, the critters play,
With squirrels that dance and frogs that sway.
A raccoon lost his map, oh what a sight,
He took a long nap instead of flight.

A hedgehog brought snacks, oh what a feast,\nWhile rabbits made soup, a springtime beast.
The flowers laughed loud with petals so bright,
As bees told their tales, buzzing with delight.

Nature Holds the Story's Heart.

The trees whispered secrets to the breeze,
While ants had a party, doing just as they please.
Beneath the green vines, a turtle spun round,
While a parrot rehearsed its best silly sound.

A monkey on branches played hide and seek,
While a sleepy old lizard just wanted to peek.
They laughed and they chirped, under skies so blue,
In this fruity playground, where fun just grew.

Verdant Dreams in Whispering Shadows

Where shadows play tricks and sunlight sneaks,
The flowers all giggle, oh the joy that speaks.
A butterfly danced in a whimsical loop,
While the bunnies all juggled, a wild little troupe.

Frogs croaked in tune with a beat so fine,
While a snake slipped and slid down a vine.
They shared silly stories as night turned to day,
In this leafy abode where laughter would stay.

Secrets Among the Leaves

High in the branches, the owls wore their laughs,
Sharing wisecracks with a troupe of young giraffes.
The daisies spun tales of spring's wild affair,
While turtles cracked jokes that made all stop and stare.

There's mischief afoot in this verdant domain,
With raccoons in capes, playing superhero games.
They gather at dusk beneath stars' shining lights,
To swap funny stories and share silly sights.

Luminescence of the Leafy Heart

In a pot lived a strange green beast,
With a tiny crown, it thought it was the least.
It danced in the sun, doing pirouettes,
While the cat threw shade, with no sun regrets.

The dust bunnies laughed, in a fluffy brigade,
As the poor little plant displayed its charade.
With twirling fronds and a leaf so spry,
It sought friends above, but just met the fly.

One day in a dream, it wore a top hat,
And threw a grand ball for each critter and cat.
Yet the guests all just sat, munching on cake,
And the plant, in despair, thought of how to escape.

Nature's Ink in Every Fiber

In a corner, a cactus grinned wide with glee,
Doodling notes of delight on a leaf from a tree.
The squirrel frowned hard, saying, 'That's not fair,
I can't even draw, I've no hands to spare!'

The fern sang a tune with a voice like a song,
While the spider spun webs, weaving legacies long.
A cactus can write while the oak just takes naps,
Their arguments echoed in dips and mishaps.

Then one winter's night when the moon was quite bright,
They planned a grand show, but forgot the spotlight.
So they danced in the dark, a spontaneous jest,
While the houseplants just watched, bemused by the quest.

Flora's Forgotten Chambers

In a vase sat a daisy, plotting a scheme,
To escape from the sunlight, pursue her great dream.
She whispered to roses, 'Let's stage a coup!'
But the tulips just giggled, and said, 'We can't too!'

The geraniums turned, with a frown on each leaf,
'We can't leave this pot; it's our source of relief!'
But the daisy just winked, full of mischief and hope,
Ready to leap like a wide-eyed antelope.

They made a grand plan by the light of the moon,
With petals and laughter, they felt so immune.
Yet when morning came, to their shock and dismay,
They found that the gardener had taken away!

The Forest Whisperer's Tale

In a corner of the shelf, where no sunlight dare tread,
Lived a wise, old fern with a crown on its head.
'Gather round, my friends!' it did cheerfully say,
'Let me tell you a joke in a leafy way!'

The jungle of books chuckled, shaking their spines,
As the old fern spun tales of great bumbles and vines.
'Once a banana ran races, thinking it could fly,
But it tripped on a peel, and oh, how it did cry!'

A cactus shot cactus needles in hilarious glee,
As the books scratched their covers, all laughing with glee.
'For here in this corner, under layers of dust,
We find joy in our friends, and in laughter we trust!'

Shadows of the Forgotten Grove

In the corner, shadows play,
Whispering secrets of yesterday.
A rabbit's hat and a sneaky gnome,
Once called this shelf their quirky home.

With a cackle and a cheeky grin,
A squirrel skips, trying to fit in.
He juggles acorns, oh what a sight,
In the dimness of shimmering light.

Fairies giggle, hiding behind,
Dusty volumes they've left behind.
A book about dancing frogs and mice,
Where mischief and mayhem feel so nice.

So let's gather 'round this leafy tale,
And check if the shelves might simply sail.
Into a world both wild and free,
Where laughter grows like a blooming tree.

Leaves of Lurking Legends

On a shelf where oddities sprout,
A dragon sneezes, without a doubt.
They tickle each other with leafy sprees,
Spreading giggles upon the breeze.

A bookworm donning spectacles wide,
Reads stories of critters that often hide.
Chasing tales on a winding vine,
With every twist, they sip sweet wine.

Ogre roast on a rainbow plate,
How can friends ever be late?
Join the feast of whimsical lore,
As laughter rings out behind the door.

And when dusk falls, shadows will greet,
A dance of critters with lightning feet.
Swing and sway with their friendly cheer,
In a land where nonsense is ever near.

A Tapestry of Twists and Branches

Upon this shelf, we weave and spin,
With tales of mischief just tucked in.
Knights in pjs and crowns made of cheese,
Making merry with giggling geese.

Pirates waddle with treasure maps,
Searching for coins amidst all the naps.
A hearty laugh bursts through the air,
As tortoises race without a care.

Dancing mushrooms, oh what a sight,
In this parade, everything feels right.
Chasing shadows on a joyful quest,
Where silliness is always the best.

What tales unfold as night draws near,
The woodland critters all take a cheer.
In this tapestry, woven tight,
The magic of fun shines ever bright.

Unseen Secrets of the Verdant Shelf

In the heart of this leafy maze,
Where oddball friends enjoy their days.
A wise owl sweeps in with a wink,
And nudges the squirrel to rethink.

Under the leaves, a mystery waits,
A band of frogs with kooky plates.
They croak a tune to the squeeze of a lime,
As lizards dance to the rhythm of rhyme.

The riddle of roots weaves tales so grand,
Of misfit critters across the land.
With laughter stitched in every seam,
Who knew a shelf could hold such a dream?

So if you venture down this path,
You'll find that fun is the heart's true math.
In whispers, the shelf will call your name,
Inviting you to join the game.

Pages Paved with Moss

On tomes where critters play and roam,
A caterpillar calls it home.
With raccoons writing stories in glee,
They argue who ate last night's brie.

A spider spins webs of funny tales,
While frogs hop in, avoiding scales.
The books are cozy, soft and green,
In this land where no one's seen.

Snakes slither through chapters so sly,
And squirrels debate what to buy.
Some pages flip with sunlit cheer,
A library filled with chatter clear.

Laughter echoes from shelf to shelf,
In a world that's stacked to the hilt, like a self.
The moss grows thick, a plush delight,
In this woodland of words, all day and night.

Scribes of the Rainforest

The parrot types with colorful flair,
Grabbing a word here and there.
The monkeys swing as they write their prose,
And giggle at where the sentence goes.

This scroll's a banquet for every beast,
A pizza pie, or a giant feast.
The jaguar with its paws so deft,
Scribbles notes but leaves out the rest.

The tapir hums a gentle tune,
While sloths debate under the moon.
Each leaf bears witness to fun and jest,
In this hub of giggles, truly the best.

With ink made from nectar so sweet,
The chronicles of chaos complete.
Scribes of a realm where humor reigns,
Weaving laughter through the vines and chains.

Kinship of the Leaves

Under the canopy, whispers abound,
As leaves gossip—silly sounds.
The oak is boastful, the elm is shy,
Each one sharing tales that fly.

Raccoons break in for tea and chat,
While mockingbirds laugh atop, how 'bout that?
Vines twist like dancers in a row,
As breezes carry stories to and fro.

Caterpillars boast of their future plans,
While ants put together silly clans.
In this leafy world, bonds are formed,
Where every creature feels transformed.

Together they dream of sunlit glades,
With friendships strong, not easily swayed.
In this kinship of green, pride they lend,
Nature's humor, a twist with each bend.

Deep Roots in Dusty Tomes

In the corners where shadows dance,
There are books with tales of chance.
Roots dive deep through the pages drawn,
Where stories sprout at the crack of dawn.

The old bookworm gives a hearty laugh,
Reciting verses like an old giraffe.
As pollen drifts from a sly old bee,
Every word is life's jubilee.

The covers hold secrets, a playful jive,
Entwined tales of how creatures thrive.
A lizard dressed in a dusty coat,
Composes songs that make one float.

Let's read aloud till we tumble and fall,
In this land where every laugh echoes tall.
Dusty tomes with roots intertwined,
Knowledge and humor perfectly aligned.

Vines Entwined with Momentary Memories

In the nook, a plant does dance,
Its leaves swirl like a romancing chance.
A spider dreams of a grand ballet,
While a gnome stares, wishing to play.

Tiny critters navigate the way,
Searching for snacks in the potpourri fray.
A frog croaks jokes, a real wise guy,
While sunflowers giggle and wave goodbye.

Seas of green, where mysteries bloom,
Each potted friend sings like a cartoon.
Squirrels debate on what is the best,
Nutty adventures, a comical quest.

In this kingdom where humor thrives,
Every sprout is full of jive.
With vines that loop and twist in delight,
Memories sprout, oh, what a sight!

Chronicles of the Verdant Realm

Among the greens, a tale unfolds,
Of cactus knights and ferns so bold.
They quest for light, a noble cause,
But end up tangled, in funny pause.

A lizard struts with swagger divine,
While bunnies hop, lost in a line.
To seek the worm, they climb on high,
Only to slip and yell, "Oh my!"

In this leafy world, just take a glance,
Every shadow leads to a dance.
A tulip twirls, its petals bright,
As echoes of laughter fill the night.

Potted tales of joy we weave,
In this green space, you won't believe.
With every leaf a story's told,
Of merry moments, never old!

Echoes of Flora and Fauna

Whispers among the leafy crowd,
A parrot laughs, obnoxiously loud.
In a world where cactus wear hats,
And insects play like acrobats.

The daisies gossip, oh what a scene,
About the rose and her mighty sheen.
A tumbleweed rolls with comical grace,
Chasing a squirrel in a wild race.

Mushrooms giggle, in a little clump,
As the hedgehog attempts a jump.
Each branch carries a booming song,
In this quirky realm, where all belong.

Under the glow of a tiny star,
The plant life jokes of travels afar.
With roots entwined in tales of cheer,
They share their laughter, loud and clear!

Hidden Paths of a Literacy Eden

Amidst the pages, stories sprout,
A vine rolls dice, laughing out loud.
Books become paths through whimsical blooms,
Where each chapter bursts with cartoonish zooms.

A wise old owl, perched with flair,
Tries to rhyme but just doesn't care.
Chasing a firefly, he takes flight,
Bumping the plants, oh, what a sight!

In this garden of giggles and lore,
The monsters read night tales galore.
Germs dressed as jesters lead the parade,
In this lush land, no dreams will fade.

With words that twist like the creepers grow,
Each line's a tickle, a fun new show.
So grab a pot, and come along,
In this greenery, laughter is strong!

The Lush Muse

In the corner, a vine does sway,
It dances nightly, come what may.
A parrot perched, with jokes to share,
Grins at the cat, who's lost in despair.

The pots all giggle when watering's done,
Whispering secrets about the sun.
The snake in the shelf, oh so sly,
Says, "I could climb, if only I try!"

Green leaves chatter, it's quite the show,
As spiders spin webs with a boisterous glow.
They weave their tales in silk so bold,
Crafting laughter more precious than gold.

So grab a drink, let's toast to the fun,
In our leafy world, joy's never done.
With every sprout, there's giggles to find,
In this merry jungle of the mind.

Tangles of Tales and Tendrils

Tendrils twist like a playful prank,
Stories are hidden in every rank.
The fern whispers softly, "Oh, do you see?"
A gnome in the moss, with his tea and brie.

The daisies are gossiping here and there,
"Did you hear? The cactus thinks he's a pear!"
Bamboo stands tall, striking a pose,
While ferns giggle at their awkward woes.

The mischievous ivy throws shadows wide,
Playing tricks with the light as it slides.
Laughter erupts from the pots that conspire,
As a squirrel climbs through, a true pyre.

With every sprout, there's a new tale to spin,
In tangled tales where the wild begins.
Join in the fun, let your laughter blend,
With the whispers of nature, our joyful friend.

Vines of the Vivid Imagination

In a cupboard where chaos reigns,
Vines weave tales like runaway trains.
A curious frog on a teacup rides,
Jumping through dreams where madness hides.

The orchid yawns and stretches wide,
"Who knew my petals could tickle your side?"
A ladybug laughs as it rolls down the leaf,
Spreading cheer like a tiny thief.

The tendrils tease with a playful dance,
Encouraging gnomes to take a chance.
Swinging 'round, they giggle and jive,
In this wild place, all are alive.

Imagination blooms like flowers in spring,
Each thought takes flight on a vine's pink wing.
So let's laugh and play with our leafy friends,
In visions that twist and never end.

Flora Between the Lines

In the pages where green things grow,
Whispers of petals start to flow.
The cabbage and carrots plot a surprise,
As a cheeky snail dons tiny ties.

Each herb lays tales in the margins bright,
As basil and parsley join in the fight.
Their stories curl, they twist and twine,
In the manuscript where laughter aligns.

A sunflower grins, with its head held high,
Declaring, "I'm king! Do not ask why!"
Geraniums chuckle, all rosy and sweet,
Making jokes with their clumsy feet.

Between every line, there's fun to be found,
With roots of laughter spreading 'round.
So take a look, let your spirits rise,
In the pages where imagination lies.

Trellis of Forgotten Words

In a garden of books, they weave and twine,
Phrases unruly, like vines they align,
Chasing the butterflies, lost in their flight,
Whispers of stories, giggles take flight.

Underneath shelves, the puns come to play,
As commas conga and nouns sashay,
Metaphors leap, dressed up quite smart,
While synonyms hold a very artsy heart.

Old novels tumble, all looking for fame,
They trip up each other, but none take the blame,
Pages in chaos, a comical mess,
Welcome to wordland, a quirky express!

Yet laughter survives in this zany domain,
As characters joke and dance without shame,
For in this wild maze of ink-stained cheer,
Trellis of words will forever endear.

Inked in Tropic Hues

A canvas of color, a splash of delight,
With oranges, greens, and a dash of the night,
Parrots converse in a lyrical spree,
With witty retorts, oh what glee!

Tropical plants, full of amusing quirks,
Each leaf has a story, where laughter lurks,
Their roots intertwine like an old-timey dance,
Creating a ruckus at every chance.

Doodles of creatures, all in a row,
Swinging and laughing, they put on a show,
Felines in hats, all fuzzy and sweet,
Join in the antics, shuffle your feet!

Inked in hues, too vivid to tame,
The art plays tricks, it's all just a game,
Whimsical visions, forever shall bloom,
In laughter, this jungle finds joy in the room.

Riddles of the Hidden Grove

Whispers of wisdom beneath leafy shade,
Giggles of squirrels in a topsy parade,
Each riddle's a chuckle that tickles the mind,
In shadows, the punchlines are perfectly lined.

What dances on branches, but never takes flight?
It's a riddle of joy, keep your humor tight,
With giggly grasshoppers hopping in tune,
And crickets composing to a soft afternoon.

Moss-covered stones are the judges of fun,
As puzzles unravel, one by one,
With laughter erupting like water from springs,
The grove is a circus, where joy's king of kings!

So gather your wits, come join in the play,
Riddles keep laughter not far away,
For in this shrubbery, surprises abound,
The heart of the grove is where smiles are found!

The Beating Heart of the Green

In the thick of the leaves, where the mischief hides,
Laughter erupts from the deepest of glides,
Creatures in bowties, they shuffle and sway,
Each twist of their tails says 'Come join the play!'

Vines whisper secrets, while branches embrace,
A symphony plays at a comical pace,
Fungi in hats, they dance to the beat,
With each little jig, life spirals with heat.

The moss on the ground shares tales of the best,
Of curious critters and their funky quests,
As chuckles resound through tunnels of fun,
The green's heartbeat echoes when day is done.

So venture on in, let your spirit take flight,
Join in the jest, let laughter ignite,
For the heart of this realm, though sometimes unseen,
Bubbles with joy, as bright as it seems!

Odyssey of the Overgrown

In a corner, plants parade,
Ferns with hats and lacy shade.
Cacti in a conga line,
Swaying, oh so fine!

A spider starts a dance so sly,
While lizards wink and jump up high.
The potting soil, a muddy stage,
Plants acting out their leafy age!

A scattering of seeds takes flight,
Like popcorn popping in the night.
Let's cheer for roots and stems so strong,
In our living room where they belong!

As sunlight streams through glassy panes,
Gummy worms perform their chains.
Who knew a shelf could hold such cheer,
In this finest jungle sphere?

The Heartbeat of the Wild

A fern with dreams of grand ballet,
Twirls and leaps throughout the day.
While rubber plants don disco shoes,
And play funky music—oh what a view!

The snake plant serpentines with flair,
While cat grass giggles without a care.
Bamboo sticks dress in vines of green,
Up to mischief, unseen, serene.

Chasing shadows, the sun does peek,
As orchids gossip in a sneak.
The shelf becomes a stage for pranks,
As flora join in joyful flanks!

Every leaf a hero with a tale,
In this wild space where dreams set sail.
As morning light begins to wane,
The shelf beats on—how wild, how plain!

Inked Forest Fantasies

Brushes dipped in citrus hues,
Create flora with quirky views.
Each leaf and petal, a vivid paint,
In our cozy nook, a botanical saint.

The art supplies come to life,
Mixing colors, avoiding strife.
Pencil shavings dance on the floor,
While markers sing, "Let's explore!"

Canvas roots spread wide and far,
With paintbrush blooms that raise the bar.
In our tight-knit gallery space,
Each brush stroke finds its rightful place!

With laughter echoing from the shelf,
Creativity winks and giggles itself.
As every sprout tells funny tales,
In this land where fun never pales!

Chasing Sparks in the Thicket

Underneath the shelf so wide,
A crew of critters play and glide.
Marbles gleam like fireflies bright,
Chasing shadows, sharing light.

A raccoon in a pot so grand,
Pretends to be a farmhand.
He hoards toys, oh what a sight,
While others munch on leaves of light!

The bamboo clinks like jolly bells,
As plant friends share their leafy spells.
Each tiny beast has dance to show,
In sync with roots in the row.

With laughter echoing all around,
In this overgrown patch we have found.
So let's rejoice for all the fun,
In our quirky, leafy run!

www.ingramcontent.com/pod-product-compliance
Lightning Source LLC
Chambersburg PA
CBHW072221070526
44585CB00015B/1443